# LIFE CYCLE OF A

# CRAB

By Kirsty Holmes

Words that look like **this** can be found in the glossary on page 24.

# BookLife
## PUBLISHING

©2020
BookLife Publishing Ltd.
King's Lynn
Norfolk PE30 4LS

ISBN: 978-1-78637-934-4

**Written by:**
Kirsty Holmes

**Edited by:**
Robin Twiddy

**Designed by:**
Brandon Mattless

A catalogue record for this book is available from the British Library.

## PHOTO CREDITS

All images are courtesy of shutterstock.com, unless otherwise specified. With thanks to Getty Images, Thinkstock Photo and iStockphoto. Front cover & 1 – itor, Big Foot Productions. 2 trubavin. 3 – Big Foot Productions, small1, MANDEEP ADHIKARI, Simagart. 4 – ning2k, siro46, Hung Chung Chih. 5 – leungchopan, RobinE, zhu difeng. 6 – A7880S. 7 – sirabhop. 8 – MANDEEP ADHIKARI. 9 – PetrJanJuracka. 10 – Rattiya Thongdumhyu. 11 – thatmacroguy. 12 -Rodrigo Cuel. 13 – haireena. 14 – mastersky, MIKHAIL GRACHIKOV. 15 – small1. 16 – Pierre Kradolfer. 17 – KYTan, Valentina Razumova. 18 & 19 – MEMBERHS, Pan Xunbin, Simagart, Michael Zysman, Alexander Sviridov. 20 – akolotos. 21 – Chase Dekker. 22 – Rattiya Thongdumhyu. 23 – Berns Images, Michal Sarauer, Big Foot Productions.

# LIFE CYCLE OF A
# CRAB

# WHAT IS A LIFE CYCLE?

Baby

Toddler

Child

All living things have a life cycle. They are all born, they all grow bigger, and their bodies change.

Teenager

Adult

When they are fully grown, they have **offspring** of their own. In the end, all living things die. This is the life cycle.

Elderly Person

# COOL CRABS

A crab is a **crustacean**. A crab usually has a hard shell and ten legs. This means it is a decapod. The two front legs have claws on them. Crabs walk sideways.

Front Legs (Claws)

Eyes

Hard Shell

Ten Legs

Eight of a crab's legs are used for walking. The other two are the front claws. These claws are strong and are for gripping. When a crab has outgrown its shell, it will shed it and grow a new one.

This crab has grown a new shell. This is called moulting. Can you see the old one?

# EXCELLENT EGGS

Red Crabs

The female crab can only **mate** with a male after she has moulted. Male crabs will fight over the female and she will then choose a male to mate with. She will ride on his back until she moults.

The female may store the eggs on her abdomen until they hatch. Many crabs carry as many as 100,000-200,000 eggs at a time. Some **species** of crab will scatter their eggs in the sea instead.

Legs

Abdomen

# MIGHTY MEGALOPA

The eggs hatch into zoea **larvae**. These are tiny creatures that swim around in the sea and are part of the ocean's **plankton**. Zoea larvae don't look much like crabs at all.

**Actual Size**

Zoea larvae grow into megalopa larvae. These look more like adult crabs. If you look at one under a microscope, you can even see tiny claws. Megalopa larvae float around in the sea.

# JUMPING JUVENILES

Young crabs are called juveniles. These tiny versions of adult crabs usually live at the bottom of the sea. Crab species that don't live in water will **migrate** to the land.

These juvenile crabs are migrating to land.

The juvenile will keep moulting so it can grow. To moult, the crab **absorbs** sea water and swells up like a balloon. This stretches and splits the shell. The crab then crawls out.

Juvenile crabs are still very small.

# CRAZY CRABS

Adult crabs have grown to their full size and have hardened shells to protect them. The smallest species of crab is the pea crab. The pea crab grows to just over one centimetre wide.

**Actual Size**

The largest crab could be the Japanese spider crab. It can have a leg span of up to four metres from claw to claw.

That's as wide as two full-grown people lying head to toe.

# LIFE AS A CRAB

Most crabs are **omnivores**. They eat both plants and other animals. Every species of crab will have its own favourite food. Many crabs like to eat **algae** and some even eat other crustaceans.

**Coconut crabs have strong claws for opening coconuts.**

There are lots of different types of crab and they can be found all over the world. They all look different and can range from very tiny to very large.

# FUN FACTS ABOUT CRABS

- Horseshoe crabs have blue blood. This is because their blood contains a lot of copper.

- Fiddler crabs have one front claw that is much larger than the other. The males wave it around to attract a mate.

- Boxer crabs have small, soft claws. They carry around stinging **sea anemones** to use as weapons.

• The Sally Lightfoot crab, also known as the red rock crab, is very colourful.

• Hermit crabs don't grow their own shells. Instead, they protect their soft bodies by taking over empty shells left by other crustaceans.

# THE END OF LIFE AS A CRAB

**Blue Crab**

Different species of crab live for different lengths of time. Blue crabs live for around eight years, while horseshoe crabs can live for 20 years or more.

Birds, especially eagles and vultures, like to eat crabs. Otters, tortoises, fish, other crabs and even racoons all think crabs are a tasty meal.

**Otters can use rocks to smash crab shells open.**

# THE LIFE CYCLE

Egg

Zoea Larva

Megalopa Larva

The life cycle of a crab has different stages. Each stage looks very different from the last. To begin the cycle, the male fertilises the female's eggs.

Juvenile

Adult

In the end, the crab dies and the life cycle is complete.

When the zoea hatch, they float in the water and become megalopa. The megalopa become juvenile crabs and look more like adults. They moult and grow their hard shells.

# GLOSSARY

| | |
|---|---|
| **absorbs** | takes in or soaks up |
| **algae** | a plant or plant-like living thing that has no roots, stems, leaves or flowers |
| **crustacean** | an animal that lives in water and has a hard outer shell |
| **larvae** | young animals that must grow and change form before they become adults |
| **mate** | to make babies with another animal of the same type |
| **migrate** | when animals move from one place to another based on changes in needs |
| **offspring** | the young of an animal or plant |
| **omnivores** | animals that eat both plants and other animals |
| **plankton** | collection of tiny creatures and plants that float together in a body of water |
| **sea anemones** | a colourful group of animals that live underwater |
| **species** | a group of very similar animals or plants that can create young together |

# INDEX